HELP! MY SIBLING HAS A DISABILITY

Dave Deuel

Consulting Editor: Dr. Paul Tautges

Help! My Sibling Has a Disability

ISBN
Paper: 978-1-63342-198-1
epub: 978-1-63342-199-8
Kindle: 978-1-63342-200-1

Published by **Shepherd Press**
P.O. Box 24
Wapwallopen, PA 18660

www.shepherdpress.com

All Scripture quotations, unless stated otherwise, are from the NIV.

Designed by **documen**

CONTENTS

Introduction

Tray and Malcom are siblings.[1] Because Malcom received a diagnosis of Down syndrome shortly after birth, Tray, his younger brother, could not recall a time when his sibling didn't have a disability. With no other siblings, the two boys grew up together in a loving Christian home. Although sometimes they were closer than at other times, and, like most siblings, they each had other friends, the two boys played together and enjoyed the small-town life of school, church, and play until Tray reached his teen years.

During those formative teenage years they drifted apart. Tray was a good student, athletic and popular. But Malcom couldn't keep up. With all good intentions, the school determined that Malcom needed special education. This meant pulling him out of his regular classes. In like manner, their church placed Malcom in a special ministries class where he had nothing in common with the children who were blind or in wheelchairs. With all of the "special" attention, Malcom didn't feel special. Instead he felt isolated and alienated from friends and family. What is more, these efforts to help Malcom pulled the two boys further apart. There were even times when it seemed to Malcom that Tray didn't want anything to do with him, preferring to spend time with his "cool" athletic friends.

When Malcom graduated from high school first, Tray was quietly relieved. Having a sibling with a disability, particularly an intellectual impairment, made him feel uncomfortable in crowds. On more than one occasion he overheard his friends talking about Malcom, even making jokes about his speech and behavior. Sometimes Tray felt embarrassed, which then made him feel shameful. But he couldn't talk to anyone about how he felt, not even his parents. It would hurt them too badly.

As time went on, the young men grew even further apart, as they embarked upon entirely different life courses. Tray went to college and played sports, once again finding himself in the popular crowd. He married right out of college and soon had three children. After high school Malcom went to disability services[2] to get training in menial work not suited to his interests. Once again, he was often forced into groups of people with intellectual disabilities whom he didn't even know or like. And to have a supported employment worker follow him around made him look and feel ignorant.

Then the worst happened.

Within a period of just three years, both of their parents went to be with the Lord. The two boys found themselves alone in their separate worlds. When their dad passed away, Malcom was forced to leave the family home, where he felt comfortable and protected, and move into a group home because disability services assessed that he was not capable of living on his own. This cut him off completely from his small circle of friends with whom he had grown up. He now had a roommate who was angry and abusive.

For the first time in his life, Tray wondered how Malcom was doing. Out of his newfound concern, he stopped by the group home to check in on Malcom. He was shocked to discover that his brother had pulled away from the rest of the group home residents and completely withdrawn socially. Malcom not only missed his mom and dad, he had lost the only world he knew. Of course, his deep sadness was hurting his relationships at the group home, which he already disliked. Consumed by his own grief, Tray was crushed to see his brother suffering this way. He couldn't bear the thought of Malcom going through life like this. As he drove home with tears streaming down his cheeks, Tray decided to take action on Malcom's behalf. But what could he do? It would probably be a mistake to pull him out of the group home to come and live with him and his young family. How could he help Malcom?

Devastated, Tray went to his pastor looking for help.

The pastor, who had been Tray's and Malcom's family pastor since they were born, suggested that Tray should perhaps visit Malcom in his group home at least once a week, and perhaps even try to arrange to have a meal with him there, to see what Malcom's life was really like, or even just take him out for a burger. Initially disconcerted, Tray thought he could manage this, especially as he hadn't done very much with his brother since they were kids.

The pastor then suggested that Tray also sit with Malcom in church, as he had been thinking about shutting down the special class so that those with intellectual disabilities could interact and fellowship with the other members of the church, rather than being segregated.

Tray was bewildered. All his life, Malcom had been separated from him by well-intended special education classes at school and special ministries at church. And then came the ultimate separation in a group home. With the exception of their earliest years as children, Tray and Malcom had grown up in two different worlds. Now things were changing, and Tray didn't know how to feel about it all. Again, he found himself wondering what would be best for Malcom. Then he realized—for the first time in his life—that he was genuinely concerned about Malcom's well-being, and he kind of liked it. Malcom seemed more like a sibling to him. They were starting to seem like family again. In fact, with his parents gone, Tray realized how much he loved his brother.

We'll return to their story later because this wasn't the end. In fact, it was just the beginning.

Why This Mini-Book?

Perhaps your situation resembles the above story, at least in part. Or perhaps your story is different in many ways. It's not possible to address every related issue in a book of this size; however, it's my hope that the essential biblical principles provided here can be applied to your particular need. Time and again, siblings suddenly find themselves required to step up in the absence of parents. Often caught off guard, they are overwhelmed by the responsibility they never imagined having, and sometimes they refuse the role of caregiver when it is finally imposed upon them. That is why I've written this mini-book.

A fundamental premise of this mini-book is that how you view your sibling experience makes all the difference in your ability to be a faithful friend to your sibling. My goal is to come alongside and help you see how valuable your role is in the life of your sibling.

1 Value Life in the Father's House

The author of Psalm 133 reflects on the blessings of a sibling relationship when he writes,

> *Behold, how good and how pleasant it is*
> *For brothers to dwell together in unity! . . .*
> *It is like the dew of Hermon*
> *Coming down upon the mountains of Zion;*
> *For there the* LORD *commanded the*
> *blessing—life forever.*[3]
>
> (Psalm 133:1, 3, NASB)

From this familial language and sibling analogy, we may draw two important conclusions.

- *"Sibling" is a family role that lasts forever*. In Bible times, the family was part of a larger group called "the house of the father."[4] The father's house was more than a family in the modern sense of the term. It operated according to very prescribed roles. For example, siblings were, above all, committed and loyal to all family relationships. Although disputes and altercations happened between siblings within the home, they stood shoulder-to-shoulder against any forces that threatened the home from outside. Those in ancient society who had no home or family relationships were vulnerable. Your family provided for, protected, and even avenged you.

» *The house of the father served as the model for ancient society.* Importantly, all members of the ancient family fit into this framework. Jesus even described heaven in terms of his Father's house (John 14:2–3). One of the comforts for believers in death is that heaven will be like home. After all, the heavenly Father even has a room ready and waiting for those who have become children of God through repentant faith in the Lord Jesus Christ (John 1:12; 14:2). Is it any wonder that the early church adopted the pattern of the father's house for its relationships? Members called one another "brother" or "sister," and the church was a home, partly because it met in homes. Members spoke of older men, particularly those whose writings they valued, as fathers. Godly women who instructed younger women were viewed as mothers (Titus 2:3). But all ancient society, not just the church, held up sibling relationships as virtuous. An ancient Greek sage once wrote,

> *When brothers agree, no fortress is so strong as their common life.*
>
> *(Antisthenes)*

Examples of Sibling Relationships in Scripture

By God's design, much of the early church's exponential growth and stability rested on its family-like unity. In the imagery of Antisthenes quoted above, families were fortresses and a sibling culture was the glue that bonded people together. Today we still identify our local spiritual body as our "home church." But what kinds of sibling relationships do we find recorded in God's Word?

» *Many troubled sibling relationships stand out in the Bible.* We don't have to look very far in Scripture to find sibling relationships that languished, or even ended in tragedy. Jealousy led Cain to murder Abel (Genesis 4). Lust and greed caused Jacob to steal Esau's birthright (Genesis 27). Out of jealousy, Joseph's brothers sold him into slavery (Genesis 37). When Amnon violated his stepsister, Tamar, her brother Absalom had Amnon killed (2 Samuel 13). Fear of losing his throne led King Solomon to execute his brother Adonijah (1 Kings 1–2). And who can forget James and John the sons of Zebedee, competing with one another in sibling rivalry over who would be greatest in Jesus' kingdom (Mark 10:35–40)!

» *Scripture also shows us many beautiful sibling relationships.* Miriam hid and watched over her baby brother Moses in order to protect him from certain death by Pharaoh's decree (Exodus 2). In spite of his brothers mistreating him, Joseph cared for them and the rest of the family when famine threatened their lives (Genesis 45).

There are many more examples in Scripture of both exemplary and challenging relationships between siblings. In fact, God's Word tells us that although there is a friend who stays closer than a brother (Proverbs 18:24), brothers and sisters can be closer than good friends. But what happens when one sibling has a disability?

Sibling relationships can be complex. Add disability, and they can become even more challenging. But before we look at the question of disability in sibling relationships, we must first consider what disability is.

What Is Disability?

Defining disability is not easy. Some people look exclusively at the impairment, that is, the functional loss in seeing, hearing, speaking, thinking, or mobility. Others view disability as a social construct that segregates or excludes people with disabilities, saying that impairment is part of living.[5] We can acknowledge both sets of disability issues without delving into the complexities of this important debate which are beyond the scope of this study. Instead we will focus on the experience of disability.[6]

When processing all that goes with disability, it helps to know that you and your sibling are not alone. Globally, one in seven people lives with a disability. This is the world's largest minority group. Among these are some of the poorest, least educated, and most health deprived. Much of their suffering is due to the fact that they are also the least employed. Until recently, it was assumed that about 30 percent of persons with disabilities globally were employed. Current studies demonstrate that the number may be closer to 15 percent. That means that around 85 percent of persons with disabilities are underemployed and, therefore, must resort to other methods of support including begging, theft, drug sales, even prostitution, just to survive. And those of us who live to be eighty years old have a 50 percent chance of developing disabilities. We are people with disabilities!

Our Response to Disability

Try to recall when you first learned that your sibling had a disability. "What do you mean, disabled?" may be what you said or thought. How old were you when your sibling with a disability was born? Perhaps, like Tray, you yourself weren't born yet. Or maybe you were too young to remember what it was like. One thing is certain: there came a day when you realized that your sibling faced challenges in walking, hearing, speaking, seeing, or thinking. You may have brushed it off as an issue for your parents to worry about. But for the first time you may have been sad to realize that your sibling whom you love suffered in some way that you neither understood nor could do anything about.

Perhaps another day you were at school, playing outside with your friends, or in church, when kids asked you questions such as,

"What's wrong with your sister?"
"Why does he look like different?"
"Why does she act that way?"
"Why doesn't he hang out with the rest of us?"

Do you recall feeling the warm rush of blood to your face? Part of you wanted justice. That person was attacking your sibling. Part of you just wanted to cry with sadness, maybe embarrassment. However you responded, you realized, perhaps for the first time, that having a sibling with a disability was going to be difficult. And suddenly you had the choice to be an advocate for your sibling. Or not.

First finding out about your sibling's disability, then facing his or her social and physical struggles, were formative moments. They may have seemed overwhelming. It did not take you long to start asking questions like: What does this mean for us as a family? Why did this happen? But most critically: Who did this? Who is to blame? Since you knew it wasn't you or your parents, you may have reasoned that God must be responsible. God made your sibling. Of course, it was his doing.

Some siblings of people with disabilities are bitter toward God because they watched their parents struggle and because they saw their sibling suffer physically, emotionally, and especially socially. Witnessing a brother or sister being verbally abused by adults, and particularly other children, can embitter siblings against God. Coming to the realization that God makes no mistakes and that the sibling experience is rooted in the plan of God can bring relief for both siblings, and gratitude toward God. It is by God's design.

Wrong Ideas about God's Role in Disability

Whose fault was this disability? Although blaming God is one option, another is accepting that the God of the universe must have allowed your sibling's disability for his good and wise reasons. Yes, God chose your sibling to have a disability, and God chose that brother or sister to be your sibling. There were no mistakes. No bad luck. No blame. God chose you.

No one's sin caused your sibling's disability. Some parents might believe that God is punishing them for sinning. This argument often comes up in family conversation. But Jesus once told a group of people that the parents of a man with a disability had done nothing to cause God to give their child a disability. God chose them for his wise purposes (John 9:1–3). And God chose you as a sibling too. So you have probably asked yourself the question: Why do I have a sibling with a disability? Why me?

In this study, I will walk through life with you, the sibling of someone who has a disability. I won't try to sugarcoat it. But neither will I hesitate to point out the great blessings that come with your role. God has given you a unique life experience that others will never have. It can change you and make you a better person. It may have already. You may not always enjoy the challenges of living with a sibling with a disability. But if you will allow God to work in and through your life and your sibling's life, you will be thankful for your sibling and the life that you will live. This can be an incredible experience!

2 Understand Your God-Given Role

Why you? Why does *your* sibling have to have a disability? No one can answer that question except you and your sibling . . . together. And although you may not know the answer to that question right now, time may reveal to you some of the possibilities. For now, it may help to remember that God, in his mercy, put you in a home where your help is needed. Before we go too far down that path, however, consider this: God knew that you needed a sibling with a disability for one reason or another and that you could be a good sibling to that person. God makes no mistakes. He picked you. If God selected you to be the sibling of a person with a disability, then what is he asking from you? What does a faithful sibling look like?

Practice Basic Principles for Relationships

Siblings, even those with disabilities, should work together for the good of the family. This includes caring for family members who are in trouble. In many respects, the sibling relationship is like any other relationship.

God chose your sibling for you. He asks you to be realistic about the expectations you have for your sibling, and he wants you to make the central focus of your relationship that of spiritual nurturing and growth. That's a lot! But God does not ask you to do anything without also providing the resources you need to do it:

> *I myself am convinced, my brothers*
> *and sisters, that you yourselves are full*
> *of goodness, filled with knowledge and*
> *competent to instruct one another.*
>
> (Romans 15:14)

Spiritual friendship shares the close bonds of a sibling relationship. By God's grace and the help of the Holy Spirit you can become the kind of friend your sibling needs.

Demonstrate Godly Friendship

As mentioned earlier, Solomon reminds us that a true friend can be even "closer than a brother" (Proverbs 18:24; see also Psalm 35:14). Not surprisingly, those characteristics that make someone a good Christian friend will also make him or her a good sibling. If you want to improve your sibling relationship, consider the following characteristics of a friend which are described in Scripture.

» *Comforting.* A true friend is concerned about your interests; he or she will comfort you in difficult times. When Job's three friends heard of the tragedy he had experienced, "they set out from their homes and met together by agreement to go and sympathize with him and comfort him" (Job 2:11). Friends care when their friend is hurting.

» *Considerate.* Friends deserve our most sensitive treatment. For example, "If anyone loudly blesses their neighbor early in the morning, it will be taken as a curse" (Proverbs 27:14). Thoughtfulness goes a long way in making and keeping good friends.

- *Devoted*. In his affliction Job cried out in anguish, "Anyone who withholds kindness from a friend forsakes the fear of the Almighty" (Job 6:14). Few people other than our friends are willing to assist us when we really need help. Commitment, another word for devotion, is essential to friendships. Jonathan loved David as he loved himself (1 Samuel 18:1).
- *Faithful*. You may not want a friend to tell you things that hurt. But a good friend will say what is best for you, even if it means hurting your feelings for your own good: "Wounds from a friend can be trusted" (Proverbs 27:6). These are faithful and trusted friends. People who simply tell us what we want to hear are being unfaithful.
- *Forgiving*. Jesus called certain individuals "friend": tax collectors (Matthew 11:19); particularly those who needed forgiveness of sins (Luke 5:20); and even the one who betrayed him (Matthew 26:50). Jesus wanted them to know that he considered them friends although they all had offended him in some manner.

- *Helpful.* Friends notice and meet one another's needs. Jesus gave up heaven's splendor and fellowship with the Father and the Spirit to come to our world and help us in our sinful state (Philippians 2:4). Being a good friend demands a readiness to help.
- *Humble.* Pride destroys friendships because a prideful person is selfish. Jesus demonstrated a selfless and humble attitude toward others (Philippians 2:5–7). In fact, he lived with the poor, sick, and disabled in their misery. He even served them.
- *Loving.* "A friend loves at all times" (Proverbs 17:17), meaning on all occasions, regardless of the circumstances. Our friends will offend us from time to time. We must remind ourselves that it is "glory to overlook an offense" (Proverbs 19:11), and "love covers a multitude of sins" (1 Peter 4:8, NASB; see also Proverbs 17:9). Love without conditions is as rare as it is priceless.
- *Loyal.* Some people believe that loyalty is a vanishing virtue. Absalom said to Hushai, "Is this your loyalty to your friend? Why did you not go with your friend?" (2 Samuel 16:17, NASB). Going would have put Hushai's life at risk, a price he was not willing to pay.

» *Self-sacrificing*. Paying the ultimate price for a friend challenges some of our definitions of friendship. A true friend will "lay down one's life for one's friends" (John 15:13). That is easy to receive, but difficult to do.

» *Trustworthy*. A righteous man is trusted because he "does no wrong to a neighbor" (Psalm 15:3; 41:9). Being trustworthy means we have earned someone's confidence. We cannot make people trust us. However, we can show ourselves deserving of their confidence by being consistently sincere and honest. Good friends also give trustworthy advice (Proverbs 27:9).

This list of qualities may seem long and overwhelming, but we could add even more. Therefore, we would do well to remember that the apostle Paul simplifies most of these qualities of friendship when he describes them as the natural overflow of our walk with God. The fruit of the Spirit shows us the essence of godly friendships:

> *love, joy, peace, forbearance, kindness, goodness, faithfulness, gentleness and self-control.*
>
> (Galatians 5:22–23)

We must walk closely with God in order to bear the fruit essential to godly friendships. Our greatest expression of the Spirit's fruit comes in our concern for their eternal salvation.

Share the Gospel

The greatest gift that any person can give to a sibling is his or her personal testimony to the saving grace of Jesus Christ. The way that we love our siblings best is by telling them the gospel, and praying for them to place their faith in Jesus. Perhaps you are unsure, yourself, about the meaning of the gospel, how it applies to you, or how to tell others about Jesus. So let me give a summary of God's good news, something that you could use to evaluate and/or affirm your own faith, and verbally share with your sibling.

Scripture teaches that before we ever sinned in our behavior (thoughts, words, or deeds), we were born sinners. Sin is part of our nature. King David testified,

> *Surely I was sinful at birth,*
> *sinful from the time my mother*
> *conceived me.*
>
> (Psalm 51:5)

The Word of God says that this is true of each of us,

> *for all have sinned and fall short of the glory of God.*
>
> (Romans 3:23)

Every one of us has fallen short of God's standards of righteousness, but Jesus came to die in our place as the one and only acceptable sacrifice for sin, rose victoriously to new life on the third day, and promises to give his righteousness to us in exchange for our sin (2 Corinthians 5:21). Though the bad news is that "the wages of sin is death," the good news is that "the gift of God is eternal life in Christ Jesus our Lord" (Romans 6:23).

When sharing the gospel, the goal is not to frighten your sibling, but to teach about the kindness and love of God, and make your sibling aware of what Jesus has done for him or her and why it was necessary.

> *For God so loved the world that he gave his one and only Son, that whoever believes in him shall not perish but have eternal life.*
>
> (John 3:16)

It is only by responding to God's love and having faith in Jesus as Savior and Lord that our sin can be forgiven.

> *[Eternal] salvation is found in no one else.*
> (Acts 4:12)

This is the greatest news in the world! As we testify to our own faith in Jesus, we should pray that our sibling will understand and respond to Christ's love. His gracious sacrifice has purchased salvation not only for all who believe, but also for those who are incapable of belief.[7]

Face Challenges Together

If you and your sibling are not getting along, even if you have never been very close, rest assured that God wants to bless your sibling relationship, and that he has given you all the resources you need to improve it. Determine to make your sibling relationship a godly one. On the one hand, God's solutions have not changed since the first relationships in history. On the other hand, we need to apply God's wisdom to new relational challenges every day. Some are daunting. Admitting your relational problems is the first step to finding lasting solutions. Where do you start?

1. *Seek peace with your sibling.* Strife with your sibling may become so severe that you may think peacemaking is impossible. But God knows how difficult it is for you. That is why he says through the apostle, "If it is possible, as far as it depends on you, live at peace with everyone" (Romans 12:18; also see Hebrews 12:14). How do we do this? Paul exhorts us, "Let us . . . make every effort to do what leads to peace and to mutual edification" (Romans 14:19). Seek peace. Responding in hatred only stirs up more strife (Proverbs 10:12).
2. *Get to the root of the problems between you two.* Understand that damaged relationships result from God's curse upon sin, as described in Genesis 3. We relate poorly at times because we have a sin nature and live in a sinful world. Genesis 3–11 records a litany of damaged and broken relationships: God and all mankind; the man and the woman; brother and brother; nation and nation, and so on. Scripture offers hope for all these relationships. In fact, restoration of relationships is at the center of the church's life and work.

3. *Do not simply look for a good sibling relationship—build one.* Good relationships usually require time and hard work. The sibling relationship may bring some challenges, but it is worth the effort. "Finally, brothers and sisters, rejoice! Strive for full restoration, encourage one another, be of one mind, live in peace. And the God of love and peace will be with you" (2 Corinthians 13:11).

4. *Be prepared to rethink some issues.* For example, you may believe that conflict of any sort should be avoided. But conflict isn't always a sign of a bad relationship. It often merely points to an unresolved matter which can, and should, be handled in a godly way. In fact, conflict, biblically handled, may bring us to new levels of intimacy or prevent a complete break in the relationship. Paul and others found good reasons to disagree, but they usually did so in a spirit of brotherly affection and mutual growth. That is why Paul tells believers to "[speak] the truth" but to do so "in love" (Ephesians 4:15).

5. *Do not expect change overnight.* You may struggle with your relationship. For one thing, relationships require both parties to

work together to get along. If you are the one holding a difficult relationship together, pray for change in the other person and for perseverance and more change in yourself. Do not become discouraged if you cannot enjoy relational harmony with everyone. "Be completely humble and gentle; be patient, bearing with one another in love" (Ephesians 4:2).

6. *Beware of becoming self-focused.* A necessary ingredient for healthy relationships is "not looking to your own interests but . . . to the interests of the others" (Philippians 2:4). Love considers the needs of others first, above our own. Our goal in any relationship should be to be God-centered not self-centered. If God is at the center of your life, you will find it easier to love others and relate well to them.

7. *Find an active role in your local church where you and your sibling can serve.* Church can be one of the most strengthening experiences in a disabled person's life, since it offers the opportunity for deeply rewarding relationships. God intends for churches to be like extended families. One of the leading causes of isolation and sadness for a person with a disability is the lack of community, but churches are God-given communities for all of us, and especially for persons with disabilities who are used to being surrounded by people who are paid to care for them. "Accept one another, then, just as Christ accepted you, in order to bring praise to God" (Romans 15:7). To be part of a church family which accepts and blesses people with disabilities in a family-like environment is one of the most satisfying experiences in life.

3 Recognize the Seasons of a Sibling Relationship

You and your sibling will pass through many seasons of life in which your home situation, the dynamics of your relationship, and opportunities for contact will change. Each season offers both challenges and blessings. Because the seasons, both individually and collectively, bring complex developments, we can only scratch the surface of some seasons, beginning with our understanding of the family and home. We do this by answering some important questions.

How Did We Get Here?

We need a house, a home, and a family. What does that mean? Every person needs all three life aspects. A house offers physical protection and private space for the family. A home provides family members with legal status for rights, privileges, and responsibilities. As the first institution created by God, a family functions as a group of people who love and respect one another, and receive love through nurture and care.

- *God put us together as a family.* God's Word pictures a family as an olive tree with little shoots growing around it (Psalm 128). When it comes to persons with disabilities, the family plays a crucial role. Depending on the disability, the disabled family member may require assistance in various ways. Although it is not uncommon for parents to rely on their children to provide assistance for their disabled sibling, this can lead to bitterness and dislike for the disabled child. Adult siblings often tell of feeling guilty later in life for the feelings they had, maybe even those they expressed verbally to their sibling.
- *God allowed my sibling to have a disability, but not me. Is that fair?* In fact, guilt and shame can come from a number of experiences between a child and his or her disabled sibling. Biblical counselor and disability ministry leader Martie Kwasny tells her story of struggling with guilt feelings:

I have an identical twin. When we were in ninth grade on the varsity basketball team, my sister began having joint pain. We completed a season of volleyball with her wrapping her wrist due to the pain. As we entered into the basketball season, her joints were swelling and became stiffer. She then began wrapping, not only her wrist, but ankles, wore knee braces and elbow braces. We had a good season. At Sweet 16 (state tournament finals), she collapsed on court and had to have an ambulance take her to the nearest hospital for pain and testing. We discovered she had full-fledged rheumatoid arthritis. She had to go on a home-bound program for school for two years. For the first time in our life, we were separated. Her pain became so unbearable that she did not even realize she was screaming in restless sleep at night, and at that point I lost my roommate of 15 years. Long story short, for the two years that she was sick I experienced the guilt of life moving forward for me. I tried to make up for losses, I was confused and angry at God and projected it to many others. . . . The story goes on. I have counseled siblings and family members for a long time now. My heart goes out to the siblings and caregivers.[8]

What Should We Do Now?

How can we practice the friendship described in the last chapter?

- *Protect your sibling from abuse.* The abuse of children with disabilities is epidemic. Some studies conclude that children with disabilities are 5.5 times more likely to be abused than the rest of the population. This abuse is not limited to children; adults with disabilities are often victimized as well. If your sibling lives at home, or in a group home, and you suspect abuse, follow the proper channels of investigation. If abuse is occurring, report it immediately.
- *Welcome opportunities to help others understand.* People want to understand disability. Sometimes, that's why they stare. I recall one child saying to another who was looking at her sibling, "Stop staring at my sister, stupid!" On another occasion, a child said, "Don't even think about hurting my

brother!" These public moments in which you as a sibling may feel unfairness are important for you and your family, as well as for the person who stares or makes rude comments.

» *Grow up and grow old together.* Be a family. This means doing your best to protect your vulnerable sibling. But you should also help him or her to enjoy family life. Although it should go without saying, strive to enjoy life as a family that, by God's design, lives with the experience of disability.

» *Care for your sibling, but also allow your sibling to care for you.* Although it may be difficult for your sibling to care for you, even in limited ways, it is critical for your sibling and for you that he or she does so. Some reciprocity is part of every healthy relationship. Without it, any good gesture on your part will seem like a dependency to your sibling and to you.

Where Is Our Family Going?

Siblings of all ages wrestle with how to think about a brother or sister with a disability as well as what to do with and for their sibling. Some of the most difficult challenges come at the onset of caring for aging parents along with a middle-aged sibling. The demands can be great. Also, many ethical decisions will need to be made. One poor decision can put a sibling with a disability in a home context in which he or she could be physically or sexually abused.

Wherever you are at in your journey with your sibling, the future will be a concern. Part of that is because we don't know what lies ahead. Many disabilities worsen as life goes on; others stabilize with very little change, perhaps due to treatment. Some may even get better. Regardless, we find ourselves looking for ways to prepare for whatever lies ahead. What mindsets prove most helpful to sibling relationships?

» *Face the future together.* If you decide that you want to play an ongoing role in your sibling's life, it will first be important for you to have a good relationship with your sibling. Without it, you will be swimming upstream. Some might think that you can just be a part of the plan and call the shots for your sibling. If your sibling does not want your help, particularly if he or she is not on good relational terms with you, caring for your sibling will be a very difficult endeavor. We talk about the matter of guardianship in the next point, but new laws require that a person with a disability choose his or her caregivers and those who assist with any decision-making. Be aware that your sibling could make the wrong choice.

» *Understand that you can provide or supervise care for your sibling.* This may mean that you do the hands-on, day-to-day caregiving. Or it could mean that, in your parents' absence, you help to make decisions for others who will provide direct care to your sibling through disability services. Invariably, this will lead to the question of guardianship, a legal status by which you can play a crucial role in the services provided to your sibling that will greatly improve the quality of your sibling's life.[9]

» *Seek a balance in caring for your parents at the same time.* Caring for aging parents while looking after your sibling can present a challenge, but it's not insurmountable. I am doing that right now in my own family, and it is manageable. Many of the issues facing my parents in aging are similar to those facing my daughter who just entered her thirties. A book that I've found helpful is Howard Eyrich's *The Art of Aging: Preparing and Caring.* Howard includes a section about caring for a family member with a disability that applies to siblings as well as parents.

Will I Be Thankful for My Sibling?

Near the end of our lives we may ask at least two important questions and make one statement:

1. *Was I blessed to be a sibling?* The word "blessed," which opens Psalm 1 and therefore the entire book of Psalms, means "blessed by God in the eyes of a bystander who desires what God has given you." It does not describe a life of unbridled wealth and unending pleasurable experiences, but what we call "the good life," which in Scripture is often a simple home life with a few belongings and day-to-day experiences characterized by simple pleasures. God wants us to desire the good life. But he tells us that we need to be wise if that is what we want.

2. *Was I a blessing to my sibling?* No one is the perfect sibling. After all, we all go through the rough and tumble of family life, such as divorce, financial crises, and death. When all is said and done the fundamental issue will be: Did you do your best with the resources God gave you? You cannot be your sibling's savior. That role is reserved exclusively for our Lord.
3. *Thank you, Lord, for my sibling.* Will you be grateful for being a sibling to your brother or sister? No doubt the Lord will have taught you many lessons about yourself and others. Probably, at some point, your sibling took you to the end of your patience and perseverance. Siblings often do. But I trust you will be thankful for being a brother or sister of a person with a disability.

4 Do Life Together

What happened to Tray and Malcom? The more Tray looked into Malcom's life, the more he wanted to play a pivotal role for his sibling. Not surprisingly, Tray eventually became Malcom's guardian, meaning that he assumed responsibility for his brother's well-being. But Tray was amazed that there wasn't much that Malcom couldn't do. Tray eventually helped Malcom to leave the group home where he was unhappy and set him up in an apartment with a lifelong friend, Willie. Malcom and Willie shared home life responsibilities and had someone from disability services check in on them once a week to make sure that all was going well.

Tray discovered that Malcom loved horses. So, he found work for Malcom at one of the area's many stables. Malcom could groom and care for the horses tenderly. They, too, were his friends and he loved them. He even knew all their names and what most of their idiosyncrasies were. Not even the trainers knew the horses that well. Malcom took photos of each horse with his cell phone and had them mounted in frames which he put around his apartment. Willie liked the pictures too, especially when Malcom told him stories about each of the horses.

On weekends, Malcom went to Tray's house to spend time with family. Tray's wife, Linda, loved Malcom like a brother and served meals that Malcom especially liked. On Sunday, the family went to church and sat together. In time, the pastor shut down the special class and included the people with intellectual disabilities in all of the church's ministries. He even started an adopt-a-friend ministry in which people with developmental disabilities who did not have caring families might be adopted by families or individuals in the church. Again, and not surprisingly, many of these families ended up as guardians for their adoptees.

Tray and Malcom's story is not uncommon among siblings. Their parents believed that the two boys should pursue their own lives and dreams even if it meant they would not be close siblings. After all, why burden Tray with "their problems," a.k.a. Malcom. They were truly people of their generation. But times have changed. Families no longer send their children with intellectual disabilities away to institutions. Nowadays parents typically try to keep their children with disabilities at home and create a normal life for them. In fact, some parents are deeply concerned about the high abuse rate among children who are institutionalized. What is more, daily we are coming to realize that people with intellectual disabilities can lead lives of their own choice just like anyone else. They can live in an apartment with a friend, work at a job, and take part in every sphere of society. Disability services are available to assist, but only where assistance is really needed. By law, persons with disabilities are invited to plan their own lives with a little assistance from people they trust.

What are people with intellectual disabilities looking for in life? Like the rest of us, they are looking for family, friends, enjoyable experiences, and meaning in life. They have their own dreams and preferences that are very important to them. We'll discuss this important point more in the next section.

Disability Issues to Consider

Having considered the biblical directives for godly and successful sibling relationships, we turn our attention to some of the disability issues that you as a sibling need to be aware of and in which you may want to participate.

- *See to it that your sibling has full access to and is included in all activities in which he or she desires to participate.* This is a minimum standard for disability support. Churches can set the tone by including people with disabilities in all aspects of local church ministry, as much as possible.
- *Build circles of support around your sibling.* Start with the family, then the local church, and finally the community. Don't try to do it all yourself. You can't. And if you feel tempted to try to care for a sibling with a disability without other relationships, remind yourself that you are depriving your sibling of the life-giving relationships he or she needs.
- *Do person-centered planning for every aspect of life with the circle of supporters, if possible.*[10] It is good to have several groups of people who support the life of people with disabilities. A very small inner circle should love that person regardless of what happens. In the next circle should be those people who support your sibling outside

the day-in, day-out routine. The third circle will be those who provide disability service assistance. Another layer will be those who help the person make crucial plans and decisions. The final circle will be those people in associations such as churches, clubs, and other organizations. Like anyone, people with disabilities need all of these circles of support. The role of advocacy will be crucial for your sibling.[11]

» *Do not underestimate what a person with intellectual disabilities is capable of doing.* If allowed, people with the most severe disabilities will surprise you and themselves. Let them grow as you would any other person. For the longest time, we as a society have assumed that people with intellectual disabilities just need to be cared for. Again, our intentions were good. But as research has given more attention to what people with intellectual disabilities not only want but are capable of, we have discovered that their potential is great. After all, they are motivated to succeed and take part in life just like anyone else. All they need is the right kind of support.

- *Always help your sibling pursue his or her desires and dreams, not yours or society's.* It is dangerous to order persons with disabilities around without giving choices. We might wrongly assume that they have no dreams. Of course they do, but we may need to work harder finding out what they really want. One way is to observe what they are attracted to or interested in. It helps to create a variety of experiences so that you can see what your sibling likes and doesn't like.
- *Provide support only where it is needed.* Our tendency is to make people with disabilities depend upon us, especially siblings or children. But this does not help them. In fact, it can hurt them. Allow them to try things and safely make mistakes. Like all of us, that is how they learn and grow. Wean them off dependencies wherever possible.
- *Help your sibling plan for his or her future one decision at a time.*[12] This will entail considering the critical role of guardianship for a sibling with an intellectual disability. Guardianship gives decision-making authority to individuals who people with

disabilities know well and trust. These are people who understand how to find out what their siblings want from years of doing that very thing on the playground, in the home, and at school.

In all of these areas, prayerfully seek God for the wisdom you need. He will richly bless your own life as you serve your sibling according to his will and glory.

Conclusion: One Family's Perspective

Writing this mini-book has been a help to me and a blessing to my own heart. That's because I have both a sister-in-law and a daughter with disabilities. Therefore, I am married to the sibling of a person with a disability, and I also have three adult children who are siblings to a sister who has a disability. Much of what I know about sibling challenges I've learned from listening to and watching these family members relate to each other. To help me better understand their perspectives, I asked them a number of questions. Some of their responses are summarized below.

- *What was one important benefit of having a sibling with a disability?* We learned how to empathize and adapt to other people's weaknesses at a young age. Most people don't learn these lessons until they are much older. Having a sibling with a disability forces you to ask the right questions sooner rather than later.

» *Were there deep relational challenges?* We never noticed the challenges until we started having children of our own and only then realized we would never be able to confide in our sibling about the challenges of adulthood and parenting.

» *Did the additional focus on the needs of your sibling make you feel left out?* We never felt that all the attention was focused on our sibling with a disability because our parents made us feel like caregivers for her by asking us to help out.

» *What about feelings of grief and subsequent guilt for your relationship with your sibling?* Feelings of grief arose at the point in our lives when we realized (likely in early adulthood) that our relationship with our sibling would never have the depth and complexity of a typical sibling relationship. While we will fiercely love our sibling with a disability, the bond will not be the same. It will be a simple bond. Though there is beauty in that simplicity, we have realized our sibling will not be able to fully reciprocate our support of her, since she will never understand our trials in our careers, marriages, or parenting of our own children. The mourning of this complex relationship is followed by guilt for feeling this sadness because in mourning, are we perhaps deeming inadequate the sibling we have been given? This juxtaposition of grief over a lost relationship and guilt at feeling the grief is something upon which we have chewed.

» *What did you lose by being a sibling?* There is no question that living with disability held us back from vacations and created other losses. But you become a different kind of family, a better version, because you have grown together focusing on the needs of the child with a disability. At the time, it did seem like we missed out on the fun that our friends talked about. But as an adult, you look back and realize that it didn't hurt us. It helped us.

- *What does your sibling mean to your family?* She is the glue that holds our family together in a unique way [I call her our treasure]. We are a close family. But we focus less on differences and disagreements than we would have done without our sibling with a disability. We focus more on making life work.
- *Would you want your sibling not to have a disability?* For her sake, yes; but not for our sakes. She has suffered many health issues as well as the isolation that comes with not being entirely accepted in society. But we are blessed and better for having her as our sibling.

Personal Application Projects

1. Review the characteristics of friendship listed in chapter 2 by looking up and meditating on the following Scripture verses. Note that although they are character traits, they also require practical action steps. Write down in a notebook or journal what you learn and what action steps God may want you to take.

- Comforting—Job 2:11.
- Considerate—Proverbs 27:14.
- Devoted—Job 6:14; 1 Samuel 18:1.
- Faithful—Proverbs 27:6.
- Forgiving—Matthew 11:19; Luke 5:20; Matthew 26:50.
- Helpful—Philippians 2:4.
- Humble—Philippians 2:5–7.
- Loving—Proverbs 17:17; 19:11; 1 Peter 4:8; Proverbs 17:9.
- Loyal—2 Samuel 16:17.
- Self-sacrificing—John 15:13.
- Trustworthy—Psalm 15:3; 41:9; Proverbs 27:9.

2. The biblical goal of all relationships is spiritual growth for both parties. Sibling relationships should have that same goal, since we love our sibling best by helping him or her to come to Christ and to grow spiritually. In order to keep your sibling relationship spiritually focused, treat your sibling like a sister or brother in Christ. Read Colossians 3:12–14. Pick one or two virtues to prayerfully focus on. Consider writing these verses on a 3x5 card to review and memorize.

In the following list of Scripture passages the one-another commands are underlined. Rather than trying to memorize and practice them all at once, take them one at a time as they fit into your life circumstances. To start off, your sibling will always need you to encourage his or her faith. Don't we all? Another option is to pick the "one another" that you struggle with most. Ask the Lord to give you strength and wisdom to apply it to your life.[13]

» Encourage one another's faith (Romans 1:12).

» Be devoted to one another in brotherly love (Romans 12:10).

» Give preference to one another in love (Romans 12:10).

- » Be of the same mind toward one another (Romans 12:16).
- » Love one another (Romans 13:8).
- » Build up one another (Romans 14:19).
- » God grant you the same mind as one another (Romans 15:5).
- » Accept one another (Romans 15:7).
- » Admonish one another (Romans 15:14).
- » Greet one another with a holy kiss (Romans 16:16).
- » Wait for one another (1 Corinthians 11:33).
- » Have the same care for one another (1 Corinthians 12:25).
- » Through love serve one another (Galatians 5:13).
- » Bear one another's burdens (Galatians 6:2).
- » Show forbearance to one another in love (Ephesians 4:2).
- » Be kind to one another, tenderhearted (Ephesians 4:32).
- » Forgive one another (Ephesians 4:32).
- » Be subject to one another (Ephesians 5:21).
- » Bear with one another, and forgive one

another (Colossians 3:13).

- Admonish one another in psalms, hymns, and spiritual songs (Colossians 3:16).
- Abound in love for one another (1 Thessalonians 3:12).
- Comfort one another with these words (1 Thessalonians 4:18).
- Encourage one another, and build one another up (1 Thessalonians 5:11).
- Seek that which is good for one another and for all men (1 Thessalonians 5:15).
- Encourage one another day after day (Hebrews 3:13; 10:25).
- Stimulate one another to love and good deeds (Hebrews 10:24).
- Confess your sins to one another and pray for one another (James 5:16).
- Be hospitable toward one another without complaint (1 Peter 4:9).
- Employ your spiritual gift in serving one another (1 Peter 4:10).
- Clothe yourselves with humility toward one another (1 Peter 5:5).
- Do not judge one another (Romans 14:13).

- » Do not bite and devour one another (Galatians 5:15).
- » Do not be in opposition to one another (Galatians 5:17).
- » Do not boast, challenging one another, envying one another (Galatians 5:26).
- » Do not lie to one another (Colossians 3:9).
- » Do not hate one another (Titus 3:3).
- » Do not speak against one another (James 4:11).
- » Do not complain against one another (James 5:9).

It is noteworthy that most of the negative "one anothers" are related to our speech.

This list may seem long and difficult to actually practice, but upon closer examination we probably already practice these to some degree. Because the "one anothers" are important to all Christian relationships, they will help you be a better sibling. You can even counsel your sibling and yourself using them.[14] This is what it means for siblings to aim to produce "love and good deeds" (Hebrews 10:24).

3. Get a basic understanding of your sibling's life process, including guardianship. When trying to determine if you are the right person to assume guardianship for your sibling once your parents have passed away, ask yourself who your sibling trusts the most and who understands him or her the best. You may be the best candidate to be your sibling's guardian.[15] And you can always enlist the help of others as you support your sibling in all required ways. In fact, the most effective team of supporters will be made up of at least five groups (see chapter 4 regarding circles of supporters).

Where Can I Get More Help?

ABC Law Centers, "Resources for Siblings of Children with Disabilities," May 17, 2019, https://www.abclawcenters.com/blog/2019/05/17/resources-for-siblings-of-children-with-disabilities/.

Baker, Ernie, *Help! Disability Pressures Our Marriage* (Wapwallopen, PA: Shepherd Press, 2019).

Birkett, Dea, "What's It Like to Grow Up with a Disabled Sibling?," *The Guardian*, November 30, 2012, https://www.theguardian.com/society/2012/nov/30/grow-up-with-disabled-sibling.

Eyrich, Howard A., *The Art of Aging: Preparing and Caring; Preparing for Retirement and Caring for Parents* (Hoover, AL: Growth Advantage Communication, 2018), 177ff.

Joni and Friends, *Real Families, Real Needs* (Carol Stream, IL: Tyndale House, 2017).

Joni and Friends website, https://www.joniandfriends.org—search for "sibling," "brother," or "sister" to find the many sibling resources.

MacArthur, John, *Safe in the Arms of God: Truth from Heaven about the Death of a Child* (Nashville: Thomas Nelson, 2003).

Meyer, Don, and Emily Holl, eds., *The Sibling Survival Guide: Indispensable Information for Brothers and Sisters of Adults with Disabilities* (Bethesda, MD: Woodbine House, 2014).

O'Brien, John, and Carol Blessing, *Conversations on Citizenship and Person-Centered Work*, vol. 3 (Toronto: Inclusion Press, 2011).

Scott, Stuart, with Andrew S. Jin, *31 Ways to Be a "One Another" Christian: Loving Others with the Love of Jesus* (Wapwallopen, PA: Shepherd Press, 2019).

Tautges, Paul, *Anxiety: Knowing God's Peace* (Phillipsburg, NJ: P&R, 2019).

———, *Counseling One Another* (Wapwallopen, PA: Shepherd Press, 2016).

———, *A Small Book for the Hurting Heart: Meditations on Loss, Grief, and Healing* (Greensboro, NC: New Growth Press, 2020).

Endnotes

1 This story is a composite of real-life situations. Different names have been used to protect the identities of those concerned.

2 Standard terminology in disability service delivery includes "care plan," the documentary basis for administering services to the person with a disability; "care manager," the individual who helps the person with a disability and his or her family select appropriate services and coordinate service delivery; and "care coordination organization," the government-approved and grant-supported agency that administers the service system.

3 In the context of the psalm, the psalmist reflects on the priestly brotherhood using the analogy of a blessed sibling relationship. The sibling relationship is a picture of closeness and family bliss.

4 Argued in David Schloen, *The House of the Father as Fact and Symbol: Patrimonialism in Ugarit and the Ancient Near East*, SAHL 2 (Winona Lake, IN: Eisenbrauns, 2001).

5 John O'Brien and Carol Blessing, eds., *Conversations on Citizenship and Person-Centered Work*, vol. 3 (Toronto: Inclusion Press, 2011), 109.

6 I am indebted to my son, Michael C. Deuel, for pointing out that developmental disability diagnoses used to be based on impairment but now, after the Developmental Disabilities Act of 2000, they are based on functionality.

7 For a clear and biblical explanation of this, see John MacArthur, *Safe in the Arms of God: Truth from Heaven about the Death of a Child* (Nashville: Thomas Nelson,

2003). This little book provides sound biblical comfort and instruction for those concerned about the salvation of an adult with an intellectual disability or the death of a young child.

8 Private email correspondence with the author.

9 The distinctions between and similarities of guardianship and supported decision-making are critically important but beyond the scope of this study. The best approach is not to force a distinction between the two systems. Both are important at different times during your sibling's life.

10 Person-centered planning prioritizes what the person with an intellectual impairment desires over routine service delivery that may overlook these desires. It does not neglect questions about what the person needs. It simply makes his or her preference a priority in establishing life plans.

11 Angela Martin and Barb Sapharas, "Advocacy: Making Your Voice Heard," in Don Meyer and Emily Holl, eds., *The Sibling Survival Guide: Indispensable Information for Brothers and Sisters of Adults with Disabilities* (Bethesda, MD: Woodbine House, 2014), 135–144.

12 Katie Arnold, Tamar Heller, and John Kramer, "Planning for the Future," in Meyer and Holl, *Sibling Survival Guide*, 145–176.

13 For a treatment of each of the "one anothers," see Stuart Scott with Andrew S. Jin, *31 Ways to Be a "One Another" Christian: Loving Others with the Love of Jesus* (Wapwallopen, PA: Shepherd Press, 2019).

14 Paul Tautges addresses how to use the "one anothers" in counseling: *Counseling One Another* (Wapwallopen, PA: Shepherd Press, 2016).

15 This important legal commitment will require the assistance of trained legal professionals. For an example of a resourcing site sponsored by a legal firm, see ABC Law Centers, "Resources for Siblings of Children with Disabilities," May 17, 2019, https://www.abclawcenters.com/blog/2019/05/17/resources-for-siblings-of-children-with-disabilities/.

It is our great pleasure at Joni & Friends International Disability Center to endorse this mini-book, *Help! My Sibling Has a Disability*, produced by Shepherd Press. We pray this resource will bless you in your journey.

Joni & Friends is answering the call in the Gospel of Luke, chapter 14, "invite the poor, the crippled, the lame, the blind, and you will be blessed.... make them come in so my house will be full." Our mission at Joni & Friends is to communicate the gospel and equip Christ-honoring churches worldwide to evangelize and disciple people affected by disabilities.

We present the gospel of Jesus Christ to all people affected by disability and their families who are served through our programs around the world. We train, disciple, and mentor people affected by disability to exercise their gifts of leadership and service in their churches and communities. Visit us at https://www.joniandfriends.org/ministries/ to learn about all our ministries, such as Wheels for the World, Family Retreats, and radio and television ministries, and to find an area ministry office near you.

Contact Joni & Friends

» Visit our website, www.joniandfriends.org.

» For help and inspiration, visit https://www.joniandfriends.org/help-inspiration/.

» To find out how you can get involved, visit https://www.joniandfriends.org/support-us/.

Books in the Help! series include...

- Help! He's Struggling with Pornography
- Help! Someone I Love Has Been Abused
- Help! My Toddler Rules the House
- Help! Someone I Love Has Cancer
- Help! I Want to Change
- Help! My Spouse Has Been Unfaithful
- Help! Someone I Love Has Alzheimer's
- Help! I Have Breast Cancer
- Help! I'm a Slave to Food
- Help! My Teen Struggles With Same-Sex Attractions
- Help! She's Struggling With Pornography
- Help! I Can't Get Motivated
- Help! I'm a Single Mom
- Help! I'm Confused About Dating
- Help! I'm In a Painful Marriage
- Help! I'm Drowning in Debt
- Help! My Teen is Rebellious
- Help! I'm Depressed
- Help! I'm Living With Terminal Illness
- Help! I Feel Ashamed
- Help! I Want to Model Submission in Marriage
- Help! I Can't Handle All These Trials
- Help! I Can't Forgive
- Help! My Anger is Out of Control
- Help! My Friend is Suicidal
- Help! I'm in a Conflict
- Help! I'm Being Deployed
- Help! I've Been Traumatized by Combat
- Help! I'm So Lonely
- Help! My Kids Are Viewing Pornography
- Help! I Need a Church
- Help! I'm Anxious
- Help! My Parents Abused Me When I was a Kid

More titles in preparation

For current listing go to: www.shepherdpress.com/lifeline

About Shepherd Press Publications

- » They are gospel driven.
- » They are heart focused.
- » They are life changing.

Our Invitation to You

We passionately believe that what we are publishing can be of benefit to you, your family, your friends, and your work colleagues. So we are inviting you to join our online mailing list so that we may reach out to you with news about our latest and forthcoming publications, and with special offers.

Visit:

www.shepherdpress.com/newsletter

and provide your name and email address.